Affiliate Marketing Secrets to Success

Donna Piano

Copyright © 2024 Donna Piano

All rights reserved.

ISBN: 9798336395648

Table of Contents

Chapter 1 What is Affiliate Marketing 5
Chapter 2 Advantages and Benefits 8
Chapter 3 How Affiliate Marketing Works 12
Chapter 4 Getting Started with Affiliate Marketing 16
Chapter 5 How To Find Affiliate Programs 19
Chapter 6 How to Choose Affiliate Products Wisely 23
Chapter 7 Building an Audience and Marketing Products 26
Chapter 8 Promoting Affiliate Products 30
Chapter 9 Powerful Modern Tools and Strategies 35
Chapter 10 How to Make a Successful Affiliate Website 38
Conclusion 41

Chapter 1 What is Affiliate Marketing

Affiliate marketing is a straightforward and increasingly popular method of earning money online. It involves partnering with businesses to promote their products, services, or websites, and earning a commission for each sale or action completed through your referral. This model allows individuals, known as affiliate marketers, to generate income by leveraging their online presence, such as a blog, website, or social media platform.

How Affiliate Marketing Works

As an affiliate marketer, your role is to identify products or services that align with your niche and audience. Once you've selected a product, you promote it by featuring it on your website or blog. This often involves creating content, such as reviews, tutorials, or recommendations, where you include a special affiliate link. This link contains a unique code that tracks any sales or actions back to you, ensuring you receive credit for the referral.

When someone clicks on your affiliate link and makes a purchase, you earn a commission. This commission can be either a percentage of the sale price or a fixed amount, depending on the affiliate program's terms. For instance, if you're promoting a book on affiliate marketing through your blog, and a reader buys it using your link, you'll earn a portion of the sale as a reward for driving that transaction.

Examples of Affiliate Marketing

Let's dive deeper into how this works in practice:

Digital Products: Suppose you have a blog focused on helping people make money online. You might promote eBooks, online courses, or software tools related to this niche. For example, if you promote a popular online course that teaches affiliate marketing strategies, you can earn a commission for every sale made through your link.

Physical Products: If your blog is about cooking and recipes, you could promote kitchen gadgets, cookware, or even subscription boxes filled with gourmet ingredients. Each time someone purchases one of these items through your link, you earn a commission.

Services: Affiliate marketing isn't limited to physical products. You can also promote services, such as web hosting, design tools, or subscription-based services. For instance, if you run a tech blog, you could recommend a web hosting service and earn a commission whenever someone signs up through your link.

In some cases, you might even earn a commission when a visitor completes a specific action, such as signing up for a newsletter, filling out a survey, or registering for a free trial. These are often referred to as **pay-per-action** (PPA) or **cost-per-action** (CPA) programs.

Tracking and Earnings

Your affiliate earnings are meticulously tracked using unique affiliate links or coupon codes provided by the advertiser. These tools ensure that every sale or action is credited to the correct affiliate. You've likely encountered these in the form of promo codes during checkout or links embedded in blog posts. When a customer uses your link or enters your coupon code, you earn a commission—often without lifting a finger beyond your initial promotion efforts.

Key Factors for Success in Affiliate Marketing

To maximize your success in affiliate marketing, several key factors come into play:

Website Traffic: The more visitors you attract to your site, the higher your potential earnings. High traffic increases the chances that more people will click on your affiliate links and make purchases.

Product Quality: The quality of the products or services you promote is crucial. Recommending inferior products can harm your credibility and trustworthiness, leading to a decline in your audience's engagement and your overall earnings.

Trust and Authority: Building and maintaining trust with your audience is essential. When your readers trust your recommendations, they're more likely to follow your affiliate links and make purchases. Over time, consistently providing valuable content and trustworthy recommendations can establish you as an authority in your niche.

Content Quality: High-quality, engaging content is key to driving affiliate sales. Whether through in-depth product reviews, comparison articles, or how-to guides, content that resonates with your audience can significantly increase conversion rates.

Strategic Placement: Where you place your affiliate links matters. Links embedded naturally within valuable content, such as blog posts, email newsletters, or video descriptions, tend to perform better than those placed in less visible areas.

The Appeal of Affiliate Marketing

Affiliate marketing is particularly appealing because it offers the potential for passive income. Once your content is live and your affiliate links are in place, you can earn money even while you sleep, as long as visitors continue to engage with your content and make purchases.

For advertisers, affiliate marketing provides a cost-effective advertising model. Traditional advertising campaigns often require significant upfront investment with no guarantee of success. In contrast, affiliate marketing allows advertisers to pay only when their ads result in a sale or desired action, making it a low-risk, high-reward strategy. Even though advertisers may earn slightly less per sale when working with affiliates, the overall increase in sales volume often compensates for this.

Building Long-Term Success

Long-term success in affiliate marketing depends on cultivating strong relationships with your audience. When your readers feel confident that you're recommending products and services that genuinely benefit them, they're more likely to trust your recommendations and continue purchasing through your links.

Clearly disclose your affiliate relationships. Let your audience know that you may earn a commission if they purchase through your link. Transparency fosters trust and ensures compliance with advertising regulations.

Don't rely solely on a single affiliate program or product. Diversify your income streams by promoting a range of products and services that align with your niche and audience's interests.

Stay updated with the latest trends in affiliate marketing. The digital landscape is constantly evolving, and staying informed about new strategies, tools, and platforms can help you stay ahead of the competition.

Affiliate marketing is a powerful way to monetize your online presence, offering the potential for both active and passive income. By selecting quality products, building trust with your audience, and strategically promoting affiliate links, you can create a sustainable and profitable affiliate marketing business. As you continue to refine your approach and grow your audience, the opportunities for increasing your earnings are virtually limitless.

Chapter 2 Advantages and Benefits

Affiliate marketing is an attractive option for those looking to generate income online. This business model offers numerous advantages that make it an appealing choice for both beginners and seasoned entrepreneurs. We explore the key benefits of becoming an affiliate marketer.

1. No Production Costs

One of the most significant advantages of affiliate marketing is that you don't need to worry about production costs. In a traditional online business, you'd have to invest in creating, manufacturing, and storing products. This can be expensive and time-consuming. However, with affiliate marketing, the product is already developed and funded by the merchant. Your role is simply to promote the product, eliminating the financial burden of production.

2. Low Start-Up Costs

Starting an affiliate marketing business requires minimal financial investment. If you have a computer, an internet connection, and a workspace—whether it's a dedicated office or just a corner of your home—you're ready to begin. Unlike other businesses that require significant upfront capital, affiliate marketing allows you to start with what you likely already own, making it accessible to virtually anyone.

3. No Fees or Licensing Requirements

Another significant benefit of affiliate marketing is that there are typically no fees or licenses required to join affiliate programs. Most programs are free to join, which means you can start without worrying about costly entry fees or regulatory hurdles. Additionally, because the internet is a global marketplace, your potential reach is vast. You can promote products to a worldwide audience, further enhancing your earning potential.

4. Wide Variety of Products to Promote

Affiliate marketing offers an almost limitless range of products and services to promote. No matter what niche your blog or website focuses on, chances are there's a relevant product or service you can promote. From physical goods to digital products and services, the diversity of available affiliate programs ensures that you can find something that aligns with your audience's interests. This versatility allows you to monetize virtually any online platform.

5. No Sales Handling Required

One of the most appealing aspects of affiliate marketing is that you don't need to handle the sales process. Unlike running an e-commerce business, where you'd need to manage inventory, process orders, and handle shipping, affiliate marketing frees you from these tasks. Your primary focus is on promoting the product, while the merchant takes care of everything else, including customer service. This allows you to earn commissions without the operational headaches associated with traditional sales.

6. Work from Home

The flexibility of working from home is a significant draw for many affiliate marketers. If you've ever experienced the stress of a long commute or the costs associated with working in an office—such as gas, meals, and professional attire—you'll appreciate the convenience of working from home. Affiliate marketing allows you to work in a comfortable environment, set your own hours, and spend more time with your family. Plus, you can even work in your pajamas if you want!

7. Location Independence

Affiliate marketing offers the freedom to work from anywhere in the world. Whether you're on a beach in Bali, a café in Paris, or your own living room, as long as you have a laptop and an internet connection, you can continue working. This location independence is perfect for those who love to travel or simply want the freedom to work from wherever they choose. You can easily balance work with exploring new places, making it an ideal option for digital nomads.

8. Minimal Risk

Affiliate marketing involves a relatively low level of risk compared to other business models. If a product you're promoting doesn't perform well, you can easily stop promoting it and switch to another. There are no long-term contracts or obligations, so you're never stuck with a product that doesn't sell. This flexibility allows you to experiment with different products and strategies without the fear of significant financial loss.

9. Potential for High Income

The earning potential in affiliate marketing is virtually unlimited and directly tied to your effort and strategy. While not everyone will become a millionaire overnight, those who are dedicated to researching, setting up, and promoting the right products can generate substantial income. Success in affiliate marketing depends on your ability to attract and engage an audience, create compelling content, and effectively market your affiliate products. With the right approach, you can build a profitable business that provides a significant source of income.

10. Scalability

Affiliate marketing is highly scalable, meaning that as your audience grows, so does your potential income. Unlike traditional jobs, where your income is often capped by your salary or hours worked, affiliate marketing allows you to increase your earnings by expanding your reach. By diversifying the products you promote and optimizing your marketing strategies, you can scale your business to generate higher profits over time.

11. Passive Income Potential

Once you've set up your affiliate marketing content, it can continue to generate income long after it's published. This concept, known as passive income, means you can earn money even when you're not actively working. For instance, a well-written blog post with affiliate links can bring in revenue months or even years after it's been posted, providing ongoing income with minimal additional effort.

12. Flexibility in Time Management

Affiliate marketing offers unparalleled flexibility in terms of time management. You're not bound by a 9-to-5 schedule, and you can choose to work at any time that suits you. This is especially beneficial for those who need to balance work with other responsibilities, such as family or education. You can adjust your working hours according to your personal life, making affiliate marketing a great option for those seeking a better work-life balance.

13. Learning and Growth Opportunities

Entering the world of affiliate marketing provides numerous opportunities for personal and professional growth. As you develop your affiliate business, you'll acquire valuable skills in areas such as digital marketing, content creation, SEO, and data analysis. These skills are not only beneficial for your affiliate marketing efforts but are also transferable to other areas of online business and entrepreneurship.

14. Networking and Collaboration

Affiliate marketing often involves collaborating with other marketers, influencers, and businesses. These collaborations can lead to networking opportunities, partnerships, and even new business ventures. By connecting with others in your industry, you can gain insights, share strategies, and grow your business more effectively.

Affiliate marketing offers a wealth of benefits that make it an excellent option for anyone looking to make money online. With no production costs, low start-up expenses, and minimal risk, it's an accessible and flexible business model. Whether you're looking for a side hustle or aiming to build a full-time online business, affiliate marketing provides the tools and opportunities to achieve your financial goals. With the potential for high income, the ability to work from anywhere, and the freedom to manage your own time, affiliate marketing is an attractive and viable path to online success.

Chapter 3 How Affiliate Marketing Works

Many people interested in making money online often find themselves struggling with various aspects of setting up a digital business. These challenges can include building a website, creating effective ads, crafting compelling sales pitches, and handling payment processing. While some individuals may enjoy the intricacies of this process, others find it time-consuming, overwhelming, or simply not worth the effort. For those who lack the time, energy, or desire to navigate these hurdles, affiliate marketing presents an ideal alternative.

Simplified Setup with Affiliate Marketing
One of the key advantages of affiliate marketing is that you don't need to worry about the complexities of setting up an online business. The company you partner with typically provides all the necessary information about the product, including product descriptions, reviews, and testimonials. While some affiliates prefer to create their own personalized reviews to better connect with their audience, the resources provided by the merchant can significantly reduce your workload.

Additionally, the payment gateway is already established by the merchant, meaning you don't need to handle payment processing, manage funds, or deal with customer refunds. This allows you to focus on what you do best—promoting the product and driving traffic to the merchant's site.

Exploring Different Aspects of Affiliate Marketing
Affiliate marketing can be broken down into several key areas, each with its own dynamics and strategies:

1. Product Selection
The first step in affiliate marketing is choosing the right products to promote. Using search engines like Google, you can easily find a wide range of affiliate programs. Whether you're interested in electronics, cosmetics, or food preparation tools, there's likely an affiliate program that aligns with your niche. Popular platforms like ClickBank, Amazon Associates, and ShareASale offer thousands of products across various

categories, making it easy to find something that resonates with your audience.

Tips for Selecting Products:

Have an Online Presence: To maximize your earnings, it's essential to have a website or blog where you can promote products. If you don't have one yet, start a blog focused on topics you're passionate about.

Match Your Niche: Choose products that are closely related to your blog's niche. For example, if your blog is about fitness, promote health supplements, workout gear, or fitness programs.

Consider Profit Margins: Look for products that offer a commission of at least $20 per sale to make your efforts worthwhile.

Evaluate Gravity: On platforms like ClickBank, "gravity" indicates the popularity of a product. A gravity range of 50-120 is typically ideal.

Commission Rates: Aim to promote products with commission rates of at least 50% to ensure a good return on your promotional efforts.

Quality of Landing Pages: The product's landing page should be well-designed and persuasive. If it doesn't appeal to you, it may not appeal to your audience either.

Problem-Solving Products: Products that solve a specific problem for your audience tend to convert better, as they fulfill a direct need.

2. Cost Considerations

Signing up as an affiliate is usually free, making it an accessible option for most people. However, some programs may charge a small monthly or annual fee to cover the costs of maintaining the website, providing training, and using payment processors.

Some vendors may require affiliates to purchase the product themselves to earn higher commissions. This approach is based on the belief that affiliates can better promote a product they have personally used and can vouch for, enhancing the authenticity of their recommendations.

3. Earning Commissions

Commission structures can vary widely depending on the vendor. There is no standard commission rate, so the amount you earn will depend on the terms set by the merchant. Your earnings are influenced by several factors:

Commission Structure: This includes the percentage or fixed amount you earn per sale.

Sales Volume: The number of purchases made through your link, which depends on how effectively you market the product and engage with your audience.

Leveraged Programs: Some affiliate programs offer additional incentives, such as bonuses for reaching certain sales targets.

Because of these variables, it's difficult to predict exactly how much you'll earn. Your income will largely depend on your marketing efforts and the effectiveness of your promotional strategies.

4. Receiving Commissions

Each vendor has its own payment schedule and methods. Some pay affiliates regularly, regardless of the amount earned, while others require you to reach a minimum payout threshold before releasing funds. Payment intervals can vary, with some vendors paying instantly, weekly, bi-monthly, monthly, or quarterly.

The payment method also varies by vendor, with options including:
Check by mail
PayPal
Direct deposit
Payment via debit card
Courier services like Federal Express

It's important to review the payment terms of each program to understand when and how you'll receive your earnings.

5. Tracking Sales

When you sign up for an affiliate program, you're assigned a unique ID that is embedded in your affiliate links. This ID is crucial for tracking sales and ensuring you receive credit for the transactions you generate.

For example, if you partner with a company like www.letsgodecocrazy.com and choose the username "zigzag," your affiliate link might look like www.letsgodecocrazy.com/zigzag or http://zigzag.letsgodecocrazy.com. Alternatively, some companies may assign you a more complex tracking link consisting of numbers and letters. Regardless of the format, this unique URL is what you'll use to direct traffic to the merchant's site. When someone makes a purchase through your link, you earn a commission.

6. Sign-Up Process

Finding the right affiliate program involves research. Once you've identified a program that aligns with your niche, visit the company's website and look for links labeled "Affiliates," "Join Affiliate Program," or "Partners Program." Carefully read the terms and conditions to understand the rules and commission rates.

If you agree with the terms, you can usually sign up by filling out an online form. Some programs may require you to provide additional information, such as your Social Security number, for tax reporting purposes. Be sure to provide all necessary details to avoid delays in receiving your commissions.

7. Marketing Strategies

Effective marketing is key to your success as an affiliate marketer. Depending on your strengths and preferences, you can choose from a variety of promotional methods:

Blogging: If you enjoy writing, consider creating blog posts that highlight the benefits of the product or service you're promoting. Include your affiliate link within the content to drive traffic to the merchant's site.

Videos: For those who prefer visual content, creating videos can be a powerful way to engage your audience. Explain the product's benefits and include your affiliate link in the video description.

Articles: Writing articles for submission to directories is another effective way to promote products. Be sure to include your affiliate link and focus on the product's benefits.

Social Media: Leverage social media platforms like Facebook, Twitter, and LinkedIn to share your affiliate links. Create posts that explain why you recommend the product and how it can benefit your followers.

Solo Ads: If you have access to an email list or can find a relevant one, solo ads can be an effective way to promote your affiliate products directly to a targeted audience.

Affiliate marketing is a versatile and accessible way to earn money online, offering a range of opportunities for those who prefer a more hands-off approach to running a business. By selecting the right products, understanding the cost structures, and effectively marketing to your audience, you can build a successful affiliate marketing business that generates income with minimal upfront investment and ongoing effort. Whether you're looking to supplement your income or create a full-time online business, affiliate marketing provides the tools and flexibility to achieve your financial goals.

Chapter 4 Getting Started with Affiliate Marketing

Now that you have a solid understanding of affiliate marketing and how it operates, you might be considering diving into this lucrative field. If you believe affiliate marketing could work for you, read the essential steps to get started.

1. Choose the Right Niche

Selecting the right niche is the first and most crucial step in your affiliate marketing journey. Your niche is the specific area or topic that your affiliate website or blog will focus on. When choosing a niche, consider the type of products you want to promote. Ideally, these products should align with your interests and be relevant to the content you already create, especially if you plan to integrate affiliate links into an existing blog.

Key Considerations:

Relevance: Choose products that are closely related to your niche or blog topic. For example, if your blog is about health and fitness, promoting fitness equipment or supplements would be a natural fit.

Profitability: While relevance is important, you should also consider the earning potential of the products. Look for products with a good commission rate and strong demand within your niche.

Flexibility: Remember, you're not locked into promoting a single product or service. If a product isn't performing well, you can always switch to a different one. The goal is to find well-paying products that provide real value to your audience.

2. Select the Right Affiliate Program

Once you've identified your niche, the next step is to find affiliate programs that offer quality products with favorable commission structures. Not all affiliate programs are created equal, so it's important to research and select ones that align with your goals.

Things to Look For:

Reputation: Partner with reputable companies that offer reliable products and have a history of paying affiliates on time.

Commission Rates: While high commissions can be appealing, they shouldn't be the only factor in your decision. Ensure the products are high-quality and relevant to your audience.

Support and Resources: Some affiliate programs offer additional resources such as marketing materials, training, and customer support, which can be incredibly helpful, especially if you're new to affiliate marketing.

3. Plan the Right Strategy

A well-thought-out promotional strategy is essential for success in affiliate marketing. Start by defining your target audience and understanding their needs and interests. This knowledge will help you create content that resonates with them and drives traffic to your site.

Strategic Tips:

Content Creation: Develop content that is not only informative but also engaging and relevant to your audience's interests. Whether it's blog posts, videos, or social media content, make sure it adds value and subtly integrates your affiliate links.

Creative Placement: Place your affiliate links strategically within your content. For example, you can include them in product reviews, how-to guides, or within a compelling call-to-action. The key is to make the links feel like a natural part of the content, rather than forced or overly promotional.

SEO Optimization: Optimize your content for search engines to increase organic traffic. Research keywords related to your niche and incorporate them into your content to improve your search engine ranking.

4. Drive Traffic to Your Site

Bringing traffic to your site is crucial for generating affiliate sales. While content is king, traffic is the lifeblood of any successful affiliate marketing strategy. The more visitors you can attract, the higher your chances of earning commissions.

Traffic-Building Strategies:

SEO and Organic Search: Optimize your site and content for search engines to attract organic traffic. Focus on creating high-quality, keyword-rich content that ranks well on Google and other search engines.

Social Media: Leverage social media platforms to share your content and reach a broader audience. Engaging with your followers and sharing valuable insights can drive traffic to your site.

Email Marketing: Build an email list of subscribers interested in your niche. Regularly send them informative newsletters that include affiliate links, encouraging them to visit your site and make purchases.

Paid Advertising: Consider investing in paid advertising such as Google Ads or social media ads to boost your traffic. Targeted ads can bring highly relevant visitors to your site, increasing the likelihood of conversions.

5. Focus on Conversions, Not Just Traffic

While driving traffic is essential, converting that traffic into sales is what ultimately matters. Even if you have thousands of visitors, it won't make a difference unless they take action and click on your affiliate links.

Conversion Tips:

Compelling Content: Your content should not only attract visitors but also persuade them to take action. Use clear calls-to-action (CTAs) that guide your audience towards clicking your affiliate links.

Trust and Credibility: Build trust with your audience by providing honest reviews and only promoting products you truly believe in. The more your audience trusts you, the more likely they are to follow your recommendations.

A/B Testing: Experiment with different types of content, CTAs, and link placements to see what works best. Use A/B testing to refine your approach and improve conversion rates.

Additional Tips for Long-Term Success

Stay Informed: The digital landscape is constantly evolving. Stay updated on the latest trends, tools, and strategies in affiliate marketing to keep your business competitive.

Diversify Your Income Streams: Don't rely on a single product or affiliate program. Diversify by promoting multiple products across different niches to mitigate risks and maximize earnings.

Monitor Your Performance: Use analytics tools to track your traffic, clicks, and conversions. Understanding what works and what doesn't will help you refine your strategy and improve your results over time.

By following these steps and continually refining your approach, you can build a successful affiliate marketing business that not only generates income but also provides valuable solutions to your audience's needs.

Chapter 5 How To Find Affiliate Programs

Before you can launch your affiliate website, it's crucial to research the available affiliate programs. Most programs feature directories categorized by subject, allowing you to explore the various products on offer.

ClickBank

ClickBank is a leading marketplace for digital products such as eBooks and software. It hosts thousands of products across diverse categories, including:
Computers/Internet
Software & Services
Arts & Entertainment
Health & Fitness
Business/Investing
Games
Cooking/Foods
Parenting
Politics

Many of these products are written in a "how-to" format, designed to help users solve specific problems. Because digital products like software and eBooks have no manufacturing costs, commissions can be quite high, typically ranging from 50% to 70%.

You can earn money on ClickBank in two main ways:

Create Your Own Products: By setting up a vendor account, you can list and sell your products. You decide the pricing and the commission you offer to affiliates. If your product is appealing, you might attract multiple affiliates to promote it. ClickBank manages the transactions and distributes commissions automatically.

Promote Existing Products: If you prefer not to create products, you can simply promote those already listed on ClickBank. This allows you to earn commissions without the hassle of product development.

When browsing ClickBank, you'll encounter several important statistics, including:

Initial $/Sale: The amount you earn per sale.

Avg %/Sale: The percentage of the sale price you will receive.

Avg Rebill Total: Additional earnings from recurring billing, such as monthly membership fees.

Avg %/Rebill: The average commission rate for products with recurring billing.

Gravity: Indicates the popularity of a product based on how many affiliates are selling it. A higher gravity suggests strong sales activity.

To sign up for ClickBank, simply click the "Sign Up" link at the top of the page, provide the requested details, and follow the instructions. Once registered, you'll receive your ClickBank ID, allowing you to promote products on the network. When you find a product you want to promote, click the "Promote" link, enter your ID, and your unique affiliate link (HopLink) will be created.

Commission Junction Marketplace

The Commission Junction (CJ) Marketplace offers extensive opportunities for advertisers and high rewards for publishers. Here's how it works for each group:

Advertisers: Utilize CJ's reporting tools to create effective calls to action, define program terms, review publisher applications, and analyze program performance. CJU Online provides educational resources to connect advertisers with publishers and share the latest industry news.

Publishers: Apply to join various programs and gain access to a wide range of links and inventory. You can then incorporate these offers on your site, in email campaigns, or in search listings.

Finding Affiliate Programs Outside Networks

There are affiliate programs that operate independently from larger networks, and discovering them can be a bit more challenging. If you come across a potential program, consider contacting the merchant directly to inquire about affiliate opportunities.

Some programs may be "invite-only," restricting entry to individuals who have purchased their product or who meet specific criteria based on a review process.

Steps to Become an Affiliate Marketer

Now that you have an overview of affiliate programs, here's how to get started:

Select a Product: Visit websites like ClickBank, Commission Junction, or JVZoo to explore a wide selection of affiliate products. Look for products with a solid sales history and attractive commission rates. Consider products priced reasonably that provide a good commission.

Contact Product Owners: Once you've identified a product you want to promote, reach out to the owner to obtain your affiliate link. Successful communication will enable you to receive your unique link, which you can then use in your promotions.

Utilize Marketing Materials: Many affiliate products come with marketing materials that can help you get started quickly. These materials may include email templates, sales pages, and banner ads. If you're new to marketing, choosing products with such bonuses can significantly streamline your efforts.

Copy and Paste: Affiliate marketing can often be a "copy and paste" model. By using the provided materials, you can promote the same products successfully without reinventing the wheel.

Selling Physical Products and Services

While selling eBooks and digital products through platforms like JVZoo can maximize your profits, it's important to recognize the appeal of physical products. Most consumers still prefer tangible items, making the market for physical products larger and more lucrative.

Amazon Associates Program

The Amazon Associates Program allows you to promote a vast array of physical products. While commissions on Amazon may be lower, typically between 4% to 8%, the sheer volume of products available makes it a viable option for many marketers.

Ease of Trust: Amazon is a recognized and trusted brand, making customers more likely to purchase from them.

Diverse Inventory: Amazon's extensive product range means you can find items relevant to nearly any niche.

Commission on Other Purchases: If a customer clicks your affiliate link and purchases something other than the promoted product, you still earn a commission.

However, keep in mind that you can only earn commissions on Amazon from the country where your account is registered. Amazon is the easiest affiliate program to get started with.

Exploring Other Physical Product Options

While Amazon is a popular choice, there are countless other retailers and manufacturers that offer affiliate programs. To find these options, search online for "[Your Niche] + affiliate program." This will lead you to potential partners that align more closely with your website's theme.

You can also reach out to manufacturers directly to propose an affiliate program if one doesn't already exist. Demonstrating your influence and reach can help you negotiate exclusive deals that offer higher commissions.

Selling Services

Another lucrative avenue in affiliate marketing is selling services, especially Software as a Service (SaaS). Many service providers offer recurring commissions, which can be highly beneficial:

Lifetime Commissions: Some companies, like online casinos, offer commissions based on the lifetime value of customers you refer.

Recurring Income: If you refer customers to subscription-based services like web hosting, you may receive monthly commissions for as long as they remain a customer.

While initial commissions might seem small, they can accumulate over time, potentially providing you with substantial passive income even if your site becomes inactive.

Affiliate marketing presents diverse opportunities for generating income online, whether through digital products, physical goods, or services. By choosing the right products and programs, utilizing effective marketing strategies, and focusing on building trust with your audience, you can create a successful affiliate marketing business. In the upcoming chapters, you'll learn more about specific techniques for promoting products effectively and maximizing your earnings.

Chapter 6 How to Choose Affiliate Products Wisely

The Importance of Product Selection

A significant portion of your success in affiliate marketing hinges on your ability to select the right products. It's tempting to log into popular affiliate networks like ClickBank, JVZoo, or WSOPro and simply choose the products with the highest sales and best commissions. After all, these figures suggest that others are making good money, so why shouldn't you?

However, if you only focus on these high-performing products without considering other factors, you're likely to encounter stiff competition. The top-selling products often fall into highly saturated niches like making money online, dating, or fitness. While these are lucrative markets, they're also incredibly competitive. Promoting these products means you'll be up against countless other affiliates, making it difficult to stand out—especially if you're new to the game and lack a well-established website or mailing list.

What to Avoid

When choosing products to promote, be cautious about diving into overcrowded niches unless you have a unique angle or a large, loyal audience. Most internet users are already inundated with offers related to making money online or getting fit. If you promote yet another generic product in these categories, you may struggle to gain traction.

Additionally, ranking on search engines for competitive keywords like "Make Money Online eBook" or "Build Muscle" is extremely challenging without significant SEO expertise and a robust online presence. Instead of setting yourself up for failure by competing in these saturated markets, consider alternative strategies.

Alternative Strategies for Product Selection

One effective strategy is to focus on smaller, less saturated niches. For example, instead of promoting a generic eBook on making money, you might find a niche product, like an eBook that teaches people how to monetize a specific hobby or skill—such as flower arranging. While the audience for such a product may be smaller, you'll face far less competition, making it easier to rank in search engines and target your audience effectively.

By choosing a niche product with a clear unique selling proposition (USP), you can carve out a space where your marketing efforts are more likely to succeed. You can reach your target audience through specialized blogs, forums, or social media groups related to that niche. Additionally, it's easier to get your sales page to rank on Google for a specific, less competitive keyword like "flower arranging eBook."

Leveraging Existing Resources

Another key to success is leveraging the resources and contacts you already have. Consider your current audience, network, and marketing channels. What products would resonate with the people you can already reach? By selecting products that align with your existing strengths, you can market more effectively and see better results.

If you already have a successful website with a significant following, it makes sense to choose products that appeal directly to that audience. This way, you're not starting from scratch and can tap into the trust and engagement you've already built.

Selling Multiple Products vs. Focusing on One

You also have the option of promoting multiple products. This flexibility is one of the advantages of selling digital products, as you can easily add or remove items from your site without a lengthy setup process.

There are pros and cons to both approaches:

Selling Multiple Products: Ideal for larger sites, this approach allows you to cater to different segments of your audience by offering a range of products at various price points. It's particularly effective if you're using soft-sell techniques and want to provide options for every type of buyer.

Focusing on a Single Product: Concentrating your efforts on one product at a time can help you generate more buzz and excitement. This approach allows for a streamlined marketing strategy, directing all your traffic to a single sales page, which can improve conversion rates.

Choosing and Marketing Physical Products

When it comes to physical products, the selection process is slightly different. Again, focus on items that are relevant to your content and audience, ensuring that the products you promote are high-quality and fulfill a real need.

One of the benefits of affiliate marketing is that you don't need to invest in inventory. You're not risking capital on products that might not sell, allowing you to experiment with different items and follow market trends without the worry of unsold stock.

To cater to a wide range of customers, it's advisable to offer products at various price points. But remember, the primary goal is to get your audience to click through to the merchant's site. With programs like Amazon Associates, you earn a commission on anything the customer buys after following your link, not just the specific product you promoted. This makes it crucial to encourage clicks, even if you're not focusing on high-ticket items.

Chapter 7 Building an Audience and Marketing Products

While affiliate marketing is a powerful and relatively simple way to make money online, it's not entirely foolproof. The key to achieving success lies in building a strong audience first. This is the main "catch"—you'll need to invest time and effort upfront to establish a following before you can expect significant sales. The good news is that if you choose a topic that genuinely interests you, this process can be enjoyable and rewarding. You'll be able to earn money by doing something you love. However, to reach that point, you must first focus on building an audience and earning their trust as an influencer.

Alternative Methods to Sell Affiliate Products
Are there other ways to sell affiliate products? Absolutely! We'll explore those in this chapter as well. However, building a dedicated audience should still be a top priority. A strong brand with engaged followers makes it much easier to sell affiliate products consistently.

Creating a Brand That Sells
Building influence and trust with your audience doesn't happen overnight. To reach the point where your recommendations lead to sales, you must genuinely commit to providing real value over time. Here's how to do it:

Build Your Online Presence:
Start by creating a website and establishing a strong social media presence. Instead of jumping straight into selling, focus on delivering high-quality content that educates, entertains, or informs your audience. Consistency is key—regularly publishing valuable content helps you build trust and loyalty.

Define Your Brand and Mission:
Your brand should have a clear identity, mission statement, and target audience. This involves creating a "buyer persona," which is a detailed profile of your ideal customer. Avoid the common mistake of creating a broad, generic website that tries to appeal to everyone. A narrowly focused brand with a specific target audience is much more likely to succeed.

For example, instead of launching a general fitness website, consider focusing on a niche like "Fitness for Over 40s," "Paleo Fitness," or "Hardcore Bodybuilding." Each of these niches has a clear target audience and a unique selling proposition (USP), making it easier to attract and engage potential customers.

Design with Purpose:
Your brand's visual identity should align with your niche. For example, a hardcore bodybuilding site might use bold colors like red and black, with imagery that emphasizes strength and power. In contrast, a paleo fitness site might feature natural tones like green and white, with imagery of people exercising outdoors. Your website design, logo, and all other branding elements should clearly communicate who your brand is for and what it stands for.

Create Unique and Valuable Content:
To truly stand out, your content must offer something new and insightful. Hiring a generic writer who lacks expertise in your niche won't cut it—your audience can tell when content is regurgitated or lacks depth. Either write the content yourself or hire someone who is genuinely passionate about the topic. This is how you establish yourself as a thought leader and build a loyal following.

Be Bold and Authentic:
Don't be afraid to be different. Authenticity resonates with audiences, so let your passion for your niche shine through in your content. When it comes time to promote a product, choose one that aligns perfectly with your brand and audience, and market it in a way that speaks directly to their needs and desires.

Placing Your Affiliate Links
Once you've built a strong brand and audience, the next step is to strategically place your affiliate links.

Create a Sales Page:
A sales page is a dedicated webpage designed specifically to sell a product. It typically features a long, narrow design that encourages visitors

to keep scrolling, gradually building interest and persuading them to buy. The key to a successful sales page is persuasive writing—grab attention with bold statements, use storytelling to engage readers, and back up your claims with facts and figures. Make sure there are no distractions, such as other links or ads, that could divert attention away from the product.

Build an Online Store:

If you're promoting multiple affiliate products, consider creating an online store. Using platforms like WooCommerce (for WordPress), you can showcase products on your site as if you were running an e-commerce store. However, instead of handling transactions yourself, customers will be redirected to the merchant's page through your affiliate link when they click on an item.

Embed Links in Content:

Another subtle yet effective method is to embed affiliate links within the body of your articles, blog posts, or even email newsletters. This approach allows you to promote products organically, within the context of content that's relevant to your audience. For example, a fitness blogger might include affiliate links to recommended workout gear within a blog post about effective exercise routines. Just be sure to disclose that you may earn a commission from these links, as transparency is important for maintaining trust.

Create "Top 10" Lists:

"Top 10" lists or similar articles are great for promoting affiliate products because they naturally lend themselves to multiple links. For example, you could create a list of the "Top 10 Home Gym Equipment" or "Best Laptops for Gamers," each with an affiliate link. These lists not only provide value to your audience but also increase the likelihood of clicks and conversions.

Utilize PPC Advertising:

If you don't yet have a large audience, pay-per-click (PPC) advertising can help you drive traffic to your sales page. Platforms like Facebook and Google AdWords allow you to target specific demographics and interests, ensuring your ads reach the right people. The key to successful PPC campaigns is to optimize your ads for conversion—focus on attracting clicks from users who are likely to buy, and direct them to a well-crafted sales page.

Leverage Social Media and Other Platforms:
You can also share affiliate links directly through your social media channels, such as in your Facebook group, Instagram bio, or LinkedIn profile. This approach is particularly useful if you're still building your website and want to generate sales in the meantime. You can also include affiliate links in digital products like eBooks or even on physical flyers, using a simple, memorable URL that redirects to your affiliate link.

Chapter 8 Promoting Affiliate Products

Writing effective reviews for the products or services you promote as an affiliate is a crucial step in building credibility and driving sales. A well-crafted review not only informs your audience but also builds trust, helping to convert readers into buyers. Here's how to structure your reviews and some additional strategies to enhance your affiliate marketing efforts.

Structuring Your Review

When you review a product or service, aim for a concise yet comprehensive format that provides your audience with all the information they need to make an informed decision. Here's a suggested structure for your review:

Product, Service, or Website Name:

Clearly state the name of the product or service you are reviewing to set the context.

Description:

Provide a brief description of the product or service, highlighting its key features and what it offers to the user.

Availability:

Mention where the product can be purchased or accessed, including any specific retailers or platforms.

Pros:

List the positive aspects of the product, including its benefits and any standout features.

Cons:

Be honest about the drawbacks or limitations of the product. This transparency builds trust with your audience.

Price:

Discuss the pricing, including whether you think it's fair, too high, or a good deal for what the product offers.

Recommendation:

Offer your personal recommendation, including who would benefit most from the product and why you would (or wouldn't) suggest it.

Additional Comments:
Include any other relevant information, such as how the product compares to competitors or any tips for getting the most out of it.

Contact Information:
Provide the contact details of the product or service provider for readers who may have further questions.

Getting Products for Review
To write an authentic and insightful review, it's beneficial to actually use the product you're promoting. Here are two ways to obtain products for review:

Join a Blog Review Network:
By joining a blog review network, you can receive products to test and review. These networks connect bloggers with companies looking for honest feedback on their products. After trying the product, you can write a review and often keep the item. Some networks may also offer nominal compensation like gift cards or sweepstakes entries. Popular networks include:

Sponsored Reviews: Offers cash incentives for honest product reviews.

Prizey: Connects bloggers with PR companies.

MomSelect: Open to both bloggers and non-bloggers for product reviews.

Pros and Cons:
Pros: Access to a variety of products, opportunities to practice writing reviews, and the potential to grow your audience.

Cons: Limited control over the products you receive, which may not always align with your niche.

Request Products Directly:
Another approach is to directly contact companies you're interested in partnering with as an affiliate. Reach out to them with a well-crafted inquiry, explaining your blog, your audience, and your interest in reviewing their product. If they agree, you'll receive the product for free to test and review.

Tips for Success:
Be Clear and Persuasive: Clearly communicate your blog's value and why a review on your site would benefit the company.

Choose Products Wisely: Only accept products you genuinely believe in and can confidently promote. If you wouldn't spend your own money on it, it's unlikely you'll persuade others to do so.

Creating Video Tutorials

Video tutorials are a powerful way to demonstrate how a product or service works, providing a visual guide that can greatly enhance understanding. Here's how to create an effective video tutorial:

Write a Script:

Choose a specific task or concept related to the product that you can explain in a short, engaging video. Aim for a script around 300 words, keeping the video between three to five minutes. Make the script conversational, and practice it several times to ensure smooth delivery.

Prepare a Simulation:

Run through the task or demonstration you'll be showing on video. Make sure everything works smoothly and practice to align your actions with the script.

Record the Simulation and Narration:

Simultaneous Recording: Record your screen and narration simultaneously. Use a regular mouse for smoother movements and avoid unnecessary cursor movements.

Separate Audio Recording: Re-record the audio separately if needed, ensuring clear, confident delivery. Focus on pacing, enunciation, and natural tone.

Match the Timing: Synchronize the audio with the video, adjusting pauses as necessary to create a seamless experience.

Post-Process the Simulation:

Edit out any unnecessary pauses or mistakes, and add callouts or annotations to highlight key points. Include a brief title slide and consider adding background music for a professional touch. Convert your video to an MP4 format for easy uploading.

Publish and Integrate the Video:

Upload your video to a platform like YouTube, which automatically renders it in HD. Leverage YouTube's voice recognition software to add captions, improving accessibility and boosting your SEO.

Promoting Through Your Blog and Social Media

Once your review or tutorial is ready, it's time to promote it on your blog or website. Here's how to maximize visibility and engagement:

Post on Your Blog:
Integrate your video tutorial or written review into a blog post. Ensure the content is high-quality and relevant to your audience. Engaged readers are more likely to return to your site and explore more of your content.

Leverage Social Media:
Social media platforms like Facebook, Twitter, and LinkedIn are invaluable tools for affiliate marketers. Use them to share your content, engage with your audience, and build relationships.

Promote Affiliate Programs: Share your reviews and tutorials with your followers. Use fan pages and groups to expand your reach.

Build Relationships: Engage with your audience by responding to comments, asking for feedback, and creating interactive posts.

Stay Updated: Use social media to keep track of industry trends, product launches, and what your audience is excited about.

Enhance Your Social Media Strategy:
Focus on Relationships: social media is about being social. Build genuine connections and trust with your audience to encourage them to share your content.

Use Social Bookmarking: Add social bookmarking buttons to your website, making it easy for visitors to share your content with their networks.

Create Smart Content: Blog smarter by focusing on content that grabs attention and provides value. This will increase your social media presence and drive more traffic to your site.

Utilizing Email Marketing
Many bloggers underestimate the power of email marketing, but it can be a highly effective tool for driving traffic and sales. Here's how to get started:

Build Your Subscriber List:
Your email list is like traffic for your blog—the more subscribers you have, the better your results. Focus on growing your list by offering valuable content and incentives for signing up.

Be Original:
Avoid sending generic, cookie-cutter emails. Your subscribers want content that is fresh, valuable, and unique to your brand. If your emails lack originality, subscribers will quickly lose interest and unsubscribe.

Demonstrate Expertise:
Write your emails in a way that shows you know what you're talking about. If possible, personally use the products you promote so you can offer genuine insights and answer any questions your subscribers might have.

Be Honest in Your Reviews:
Not every product is perfect. If a product is just average, say so. Honest reviews build trust with your audience, making them more likely to trust your recommendations in the future.

Use Links Wisely:
Don't overload your emails with links. Instead, use them strategically. Consider adding custom-made graphical banners with clear calls-to-action, such as "Learn More" or "View the Product," to encourage clicks.

Chapter 9 Powerful Modern Tools and Strategies

Selling a combination of different types of products—digital, services, and physical—can significantly enhance your affiliate marketing efforts. This strategy allows you to capitalize on both high-ticket sales and the sheer volume that comes from selling physical products. By diversifying your product portfolio, you can maximize your earning potential in multiple ways.

The Benefits of a Diverse Product Portfolio

A diverse range of affiliate products allows you to target various segments of your audience more effectively. For example, digital products and services often come with higher profit margins, especially when they are high-value items like online courses or software subscriptions. On the other hand, physical products can generate a high volume of sales, which, although they may have lower commission rates, can add up quickly due to the frequency of purchases.

This diversity also gives you the flexibility to include "pie in the sky" sales opportunities—high-ticket items that may not sell as frequently but can yield substantial commissions when they do. For instance, I once sold an MBA program through an affiliate link with EDx, a lucrative affiliate program. Such opportunities can be incredibly rewarding but often require you to sign up for specific programs that cater to these high-value sales.

Managing Multiple Affiliate Products

The challenge with promoting a wide array of products is managing them effectively. Juggling different affiliate programs, tracking links, and optimizing your strategy can be overwhelming. This is where professional tools come into play. Serious marketers and large brands rely on tools that streamline the process and provide access to some of the most profitable affiliate programs available.

Essential Tools for Advanced Affiliate Marketing
1. Genius Link

Genius Link (https://www.geni.us/) is a powerful tool that allows you to manage multiple affiliate accounts and their respective programs in one place. This is particularly useful for international sales, as Genius Link automatically directs users to the correct version of Amazon based on their location, ensuring you don't lose customers due to geographic restrictions. Beyond Amazon, Genius Link also supports other major retailers like Barnes & Noble, Best Buy, and iTunes.

The tool is user-friendly, enabling you to generate affiliate links simply by pasting the URL into a box or using a Chrome plugin to create links directly from the sales page. This level of automation and convenience makes managing multiple affiliate programs much easier.

2. Trackonomics

Trackonomics (https://www.trackonomics.net) offers a similar service but with even broader capabilities. It supports a vast array of affiliate programs, including those from high-ticket vendors like EDx. One of its standout features is the ability to compare commission rates across different platforms. For instance, if you're promoting a smartphone, Trackonomics lets you compare the potential earnings from selling it through Amazon, directly from the manufacturer, Best Buy, or other options.

This comparison feature enables you to choose the most profitable option, maximizing your earnings. Additionally, Trackonomics provides robust tracking tools, allowing you to monitor clicks, purchases, and link performance. This data is invaluable for optimizing your strategy and identifying the most effective affiliate links.

3. Cost Considerations

While Genius Link is free to use, Trackonomics comes with a hefty price tag of $500 per month, though a free trial is available. For those serious about scaling their affiliate marketing efforts, the investment in Trackonomics can be worthwhile, given its advanced features and potential to significantly boost earnings.

Additional Tools for Optimizing Affiliate Marketing

To take your affiliate marketing to the next level, consider integrating additional tools that streamline your business model and enhance your marketing funnel:

Google Analytics:

This essential tool helps you track the performance of your website and individual pages. By analyzing how you rank for different search terms, you can optimize your content to drive more traffic to your sales pages. Google Analytics also allows you to track the effectiveness of various marketing channels and see which ones are leading to the highest conversions.

A/B Testing Tools:
Conducting A/B tests on your landing pages is crucial for optimizing conversions. By testing different versions of your page, you can determine which layout, content, or call-to-action performs best. This continuous improvement process can significantly increase your conversion rates, leading to more sales and higher affiliate earnings.

Selling a combination of digital, service-based, and physical products in affiliate marketing is a powerful strategy that can maximize both your sales volume and profit margins. By using advanced tools like Genius Link and Trackonomics, you can effectively manage multiple affiliate programs, optimize your strategies, and track your performance. Complement these tools with Google Analytics and A/B testing to further refine your approach, and you'll be well on your way to achieving greater success in affiliate marketing.

Chapter 10 How to Make a Successful Affiliate Website

If building a profitable website were as easy as pie, everyone would be doing it. While creating a basic website isn't particularly challenging, constructing one that generates significant affiliate income is a more nuanced endeavor.

Give Your Audience What They Want

People often say there's no "magic formula" for creating a successful affiliate website, and while that's partly true, understanding your audience's needs is key to your success. There are a few essential elements your visitors will expect:

High-Quality Content

The importance of quality content cannot be overstated. It's not enough to fill your site with generic or "filler" content—your readers crave valuable, actionable information. Whether you're offering revolutionary insights, expert advice, or helpful resources, the content must be something that your audience will appreciate and find useful.

Consider your own experience when searching online. You've likely encountered sites that seemed promising at first glance but left you disappointed with irrelevant or low-quality content. When this happens, what's your immediate reaction? You click the "back" button and look for a site that provides what you're actually seeking. Your readers are no different. To keep them engaged and interested, every piece of content on your site—whether it's an article, blog post, video, or image—must offer value and meet their expectations. This not only keeps them on your site longer but also increases the likelihood they'll take further action, such as making a purchase.

Tips for Providing Quality Content:

Focus on Readers First, Search Engines Second: Optimize your content for your audience rather than solely for search engines. This approach naturally improves your search rankings because when your audience finds value in your content, they're more likely to engage with it.

Thorough Research: Ensure your content is accurate and well-researched. Providing incorrect information can harm your credibility and drive potential customers away.

Deliver on Promises: If your headline promises "10 Ways to Overcome Fear," make sure your article delivers exactly that. Misleading titles frustrate readers and can lead to higher bounce rates, which negatively impacts your site's performance.

Create an Attractive, User-Friendly Design

Gone are the days when tacky designs and cluttered interfaces were acceptable. Your website's design is often the first impression visitors will have of your brand, and you want that impression to inspire confidence and trust.

Look at other successful websites. Notice how their design elements—layout, colors, fonts, and imagery—work together to create an inviting experience. If your site is outdated, difficult to navigate, or simply unattractive, visitors are more likely to leave without engaging further.

Design Tips:

Simplicity and Elegance: You don't need advanced coding skills or expensive design software to create a professional-looking site. Platforms like WordPress offer user-friendly themes that can make your site visually appealing with just a few clicks.

Consistent Branding: Ensure that your design reflects your brand identity. Consistent use of colors, fonts, and imagery helps build brand recognition and trust.

Mobile Responsiveness: With an increasing number of users browsing on mobile devices, your website must be mobile-friendly. A site that looks great on desktops but is cumbersome on phones will lose visitors.

Implement Effective Opt-In Forms

While the saying "the money is in the list" might have exceptions, building a strong email list remains a cornerstone of successful affiliate marketing. Encouraging visitors to subscribe to your email list allows you to build a relationship with them and opens up opportunities for repeat sales through targeted email marketing.

Key Elements of Successful Opt-In Forms:

A Compelling Hook: Your opt-in offer should be so enticing that visitors feel they'd be missing out if they didn't sign up. This could be a valuable eBook, a free course, or an exclusive discount. Make the offer irresistible by clearly communicating its value.

High-Converting Design: Ensure your opt-in forms are attractive and strategically placed. They should be easy to spot without being intrusive, guiding visitors naturally to subscribe without disrupting their browsing experience.

Deliver Exceptional Customer Service

Even if you're not directly handling products or orders, offering stellar customer service can set you apart from competitors. Good customer service builds trust and encourages repeat business, turning one-time visitors into loyal customers.

Customer Service Strategies:

Prompt Responses: Reply to inquiries, comments, and complaints quickly and courteously. Even if you don't have an immediate answer, let the customer know you're looking into it and follow up with the information they need.

Be Helpful: Going the extra mile to assist a visitor can leave a lasting impression. Whether it's finding information for them or providing detailed guidance, your efforts will likely lead to positive word-of-mouth and increased customer loyalty.

Build Your Website Right

To build an affiliate website that consistently generates profits, you need to ensure that every aspect—from content to design to customer service—is executed flawlessly. Think of it as baking a cake: leave out key ingredients or use the wrong ones, and the result will be disappointing. But if you follow the recipe carefully, you'll create something that not only looks good but also brings in the results you're aiming for.

By giving your audience what they want, creating a user-friendly design, implementing effective opt-in forms, and providing excellent customer service, you'll be well on your way to building a successful affiliate website.

Conclusion

When done right, affiliate marketing can be a highly profitable business. However, it's essential to remember that it requires consistent effort on your part. You can't just set up a website and expect it to succeed on its own. To achieve success, you need to actively promote your products. The more you engage and the more effectively you market, the more you'll sell.

Affiliate marketing is not a get-rich-quick scheme that you can dive into with enthusiasm, only to abandon after a few weeks if you don't see immediate profits. Building an audience, growing your email list, and cultivating a loyal customer base takes time. Patience is key—stick with it, and your perseverance will pay off. If you're impatient and give up too soon, failure is almost guaranteed.

To succeed in affiliate marketing, you must be passionately involved. Actively work on growing your business and focus on solving your readers' problems. It's also important to remember that doing things solely for the money rarely leads to long-term success. That's why it's crucial to choose products you genuinely believe in and would use yourself. When you're passionate about the products you promote and have confidence in their value, it becomes much easier to market them effectively. Writing about products you trust and care about often doesn't even feel like work because you enjoy it.

Affiliate marketing isn't for everyone, but if you've bought this book and read this far, it's clear you're interested. One critical thing to remember is that "without customers, you have no business." This statement may seem obvious, but it carries significant weight with two distinct meanings:

Attracting Customers: If you don't promote your products and attract potential customers to your site, having a site is pointless. You'll never make a profit if your target audience never sees your offerings. It's essential to know your target market and find effective ways to draw them in. Promote your products in a way that appeals to their needs and interests.

Retaining Customers: Your customers are the lifeblood of your business—treat them well! Don't stop working once you've attracted them. Remember, you need them to keep your business profitable. Center your efforts around your customers. Get to know them and understand what they're looking for. Consider surveying your target market to discover their exact needs and preferences. Once you know what they want, make sure you deliver.

One of the biggest mistakes an affiliate marketer can make is to misunderstand their customers. It's not enough to assume you can sell Product X just because someone else did and made a profit. If your audience is interested in Product Y, then Product X won't sell no matter how much effort you put into it. Your site should revolve around your customers' wants and needs. Provide them with the information they seek and offer the products they want to buy, and you'll have satisfied customers who will keep coming back.

People who are passionate about their niche and genuinely like the products they sell often excel in affiliate marketing. Their belief in what they're selling and enjoyment of the process make a significant difference. However, you don't have to be passionate to make a profit—what you do need is dedication. This is YOUR business. YOU decide what to sell, how to promote it, and how much effort you're willing to put in. It does take some work, but by conducting the right research, finding the right products, and promoting them effectively, YOU can be the one reaping the rewards.

www.ingramcontent.com/pod-product-compliance
Lightning Source LLC
Chambersburg PA
CBHW070952220526
45471CB00007B/2995